It's in the Loft

by Julie Taylor

Illustrated by Stephen Player

Chapter One

Rob lay still. A strange noise had woken him up again. It seemed to come from above his head. He listened. Silence.

He looked at the clock. Twelve fifteen. Rob yawned loudly. He'd been woken up like this every night for a week.

Rob got out of bed to have a look around. He trod on a book lying on the floor beside the bed. A book all about haunted houses. He walked over to the window, pulled back the curtains and looked out. No one was moving about down there. Not that he could see much, just the dark shapes of trees and bushes.

Rob opened the bedroom door and looked up and down the landing. Nothing. A shiver crept down his spine.

The landing carpet felt warm against his bare feet. Rob walked downstairs and looked in the kitchen. Nothing. He checked the back door. It was still locked. He looked in the other rooms. Nothing.

Rob went back to bed. He lay awake for ages, thinking about what could have made the noise. Rob rolled over and pulled the blankets higher, deciding it must have been another bad dream. In minutes he was fast asleep.

Chapter Two

The next day at school, Rob found it hard to keep his mind on lessons. He felt tired. His eyelids felt heavy and his mind kept drifting.

"Robert!" the teacher shouted. Rob jumped and nearly fell off his chair. "Daydreaming again, lad?"

"No, Sir."

"What were you doing with your eyes closed then? Sleeping?"

"No, Sir. I ... I was thinking hard about my work, Sir."

"A likely story. Try going to bed early for once! Understand?"

"Yes, Sir." Rob's face turned bright red. He felt as if all the other kids were laughing at him.

I'm going to find what is waking me up every night.

Chapter Three

At bedtime, Rob took a torch upstairs and hid it under the bed.

He set his alarm clock and put it under the pillow to test it. He waited a minute. The alarm rang. It sounded loud enough for him to hear it without it waking his parents.

Rob set the alarm for midnight and put it back under the pillow. Everything was ready. He got into bed.

Outside, it was not quite dark yet. Rob lay awake wondering what he would find in the loft. He tossed and turned for ages before he dropped off to sleep.

Chapter Four

The alarm clock rang under Rob's pillow. He woke at once, grabbed the clock and turned it off before anyone else could hear it.

The wait began.

Rob did not know how long it would be until he heard the sound. He got dressed and sat in the dark. He watched the hands crawl round the clock face.

Quarter past twelve. Still no sound. At half past, Rob decided to forget the idea.

I knew it, he thought. It's not going to happen.

He undressed, got back into bed and closed his eyes.

Then it happened.

Rob heard a screeching sound. He sat up. Above his head he heard loud scraping noises followed by a squeal of pain.

The squeal seemed to drag on for ever.

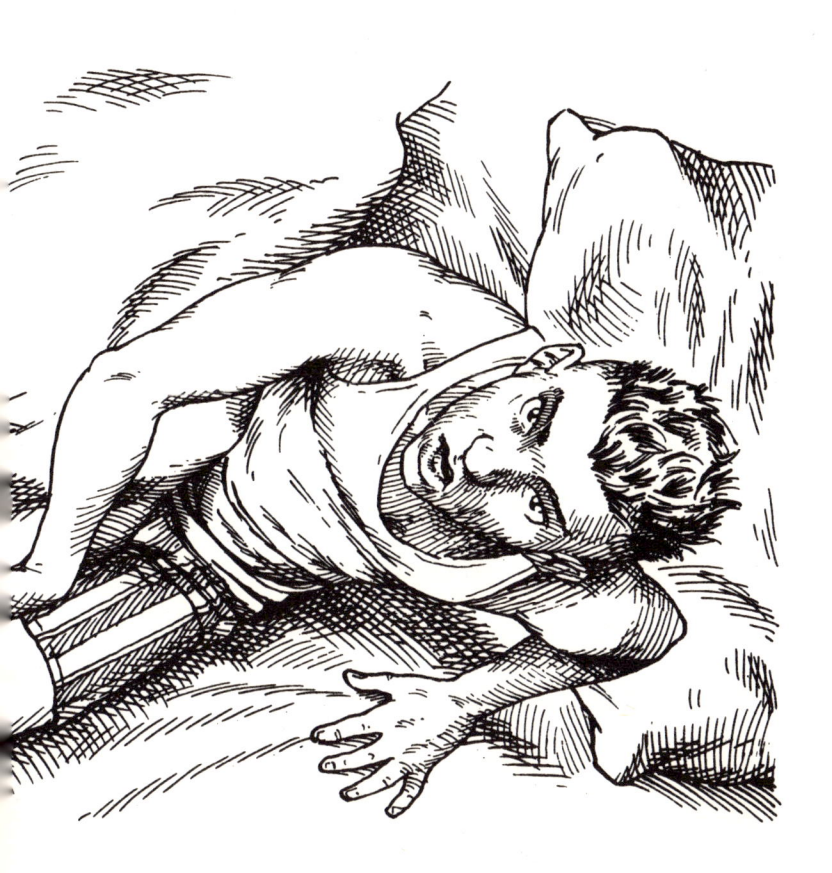

He shivered. He'd never heard of a ghost in a loft before. But this house was very old. Many things could have happened before his family moved in.

There's got to be a ghost up there. It's dragging something across the loft.

Rob dived beneath the blankets.
Suddenly the squealing stopped.
Then the scraping sounds started again.
Louder this time.

Rob wanted to cry out for help, but no sound came out.

Chapter Five

Next morning, Rob **got up** and ate breakfast. He was **more tired** than ever. He went back upstairs and **got** ready for school.

Rob was half-way **down** the stairs when his mother said, "What are you doing Robert? It's Saturday."

"Saturday?"

"Yes, Robert," his mother smiled. He went back to bed.

I should be safe. I've never heard the sounds in the daytime.

When Rob woke he found the house empty. A note on the table said his parents were out shopping. While he was sitting at the table drinking a cup of coffee, an idea came to him.

He carried a chair upstairs and put it under the loft hatch. Torch in hand, he opened the hatch and poked his head into the gloom.

Thin rays of light shone between the roof slates. It felt very spooky.

Rob listened but could hear nothing. He turned the torch on, laid it inside the loft, then pulled himself up.

He pointed the torch beam into the gloom. Boxes lay on the floor, cobwebs hung everywhere and it smelt musty. Cold air rushed through the loft.

Rob stood up. He walked in a bit further and shone the torch beam on the floor. He could not see any marks in the dust or any sign of a ghost. He shone the torch beam around but found nothing unusual.

A faint beating sound made Rob turn round. There was a screech, followed by a rush of cold air. Rob dropped the torch. The glass broke and the light went out. Darkness filled the loft.

Rob panicked.

He tried to run but he tripped. As he fell, a black shadow came out of the darkness. Something sharp hit his head. Blood oozed from a cut and dribbled down his face.

Rob was filled with terror.

The ghost has come for me! I'm going to be killed by a mad ghost!

He crawled on hands and knees to the hatch. The screeching filled his ears. The beating sound came closer. He cried out in pain as he was hit again. Rob fell head first through the hatch. He seemed to fall for ages, then crashed into the chair.

Cold blackness washed over him.

Chapter Six

"Robert?" The voice called from far away. It seemed hollow. Not real. "Robert!"

Rob struggled.

Cold hands touched his face.

Oh no, he thought, I'm dead. The ghost has killed me and come to take me away.

"No!" Rob groaned, "I must get away." He struggled harder, trying to escape.

The voice called his name again. Softer, more gentle this time. "Robert. Can you hear me? Are you all right?"

Rob recognized the voice. "Is that you, Mum?"

He opened his eyes.

"Of course it is. Who did you think it was?"

"The ghost!" Rob tried to get up. "He's after me."

Rob's dad appeared. "Dad," Rob gasped. "The loft. The ghost is in the loft!"

"It's OK, son. You fell and banged your head. Lie still, there's a good lad."

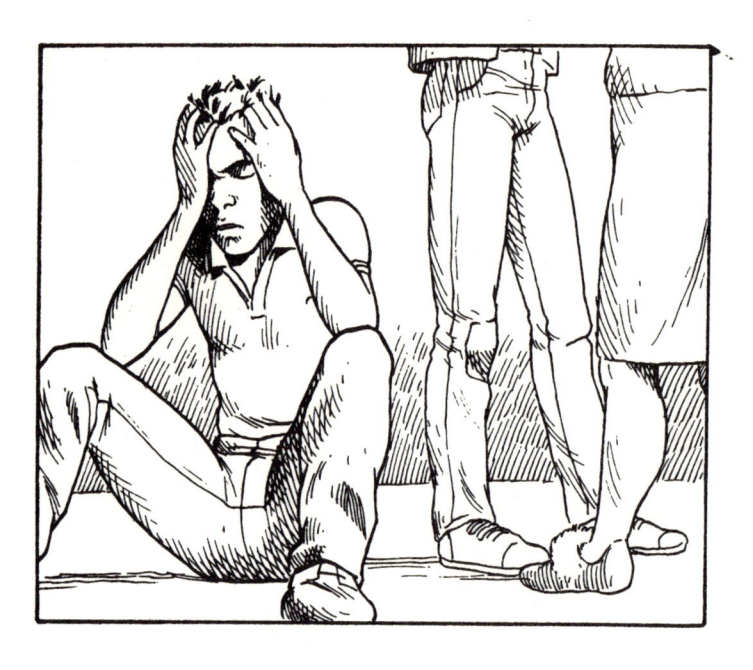

Rob's head ached. His brain felt fuzzy. The faces swam before his eyes. He closed them.

He heard his mum and dad talking about a doctor coming soon. They sounded a long way off.

He wanted to tell them about the ghost but he couldn't. The words would not come out of his mouth.

Chapter Seven

Rob lay in bed. The same bed where he'd heard those strange noises. His mother brought him a hot drink and gave him some pain killers.

"You must rest now. You heard what the doctor said." She walked out of the room before he could argue.

The bang on Rob's head and the tablets made him feel sleepy. He dozed off.

Dreams filled his head. Nightmares about the mad ghost tortured him.

He pictured the ghost coming down through the open hatch. He woke covered in sweat. Rob banged on the floor.

In seconds, his father and mother entered the bedroom. "What's wrong?" they asked.

"The loft," Rob whispered. "We must get out of here before the ghost gets us all."

"You're not still going on about that, are you?" his mother asked.

"Listen," he gasped, "Please!"

Rob told the story about hearing the noises every night. The scratching noises.

The squeals of pain. He told them how he went into the loft that morning and was attacked by the mad ghost because he'd discovered its secret.

His parents stared at each other and shook their heads.

"It's true," Rob pleaded. "Why don't you believe me?"

"OK," his father said, "I'll fix up a light and look in the loft myself. Will that make you happy?"

Rob nodded.

His father left the bedroom muttering about kids watching too much television.

"Be careful," Rob shouted.

Chapter Eight

Rob heard his father put the steps under the loft hatch. The metal steps creaked as his father climbed up them.

Rob closed his eyes and held his breath.

Footsteps sounded above Rob's head. "I'm up," his father shouted.

Rob felt weak. Blood pounded in his ears. He wanted to be there to help.

A scream filled the air, followed a second later by a loud crash.

"Dad!" Rob shouted.

His mother ran from the bedroom. "George," she shouted up the steps. "George. Are you all right?"

Silence.

Rob climbed out of bed. His legs felt weak. He staggered on to the landing beside his mother. Her face turned pale.

"George! Answer me!" she shouted.

Silence.

"It's got my dad! The ghost has got my dad! I've got to help him," Rob shouted as he climbed the steps.

"No, Robert!" his mother called, but Rob was already half-way through the hatch.

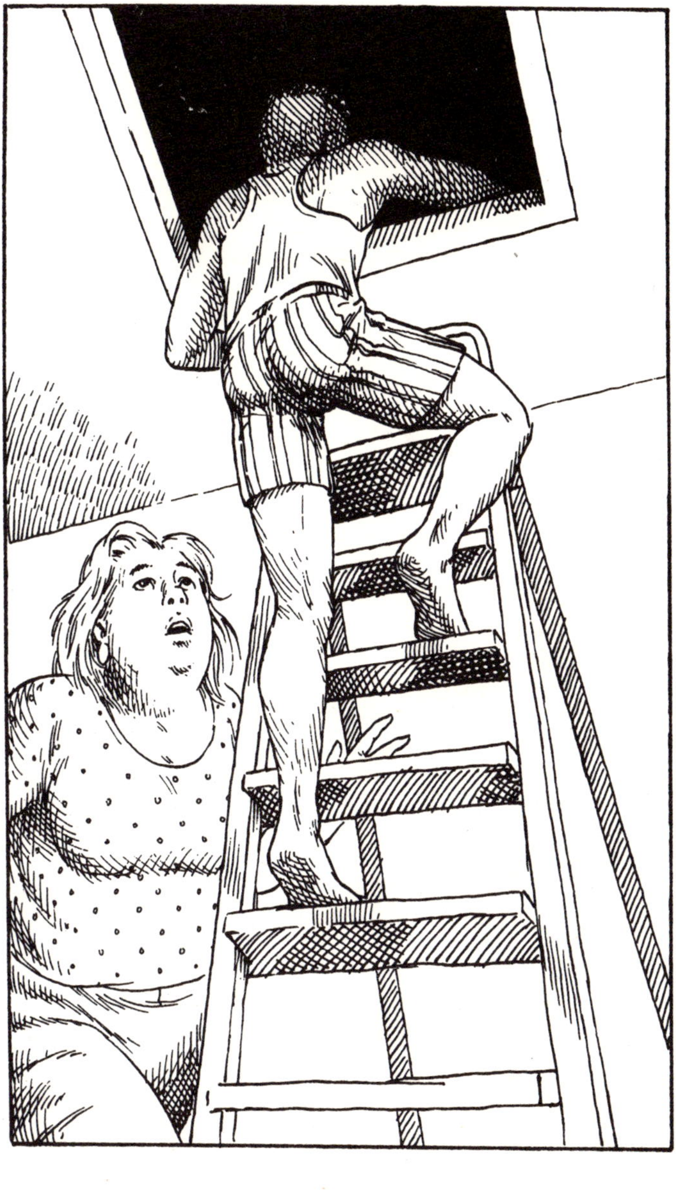

Chapter Nine

Rob found his father on the loft floor. "Dad! Dad!" he shouted, but he got no answer.

Before he got a chance to help his father, Rob heard the same beating noise he'd heard last time he was in the loft. He ducked.

The sound passed over his head.

It came at him again, out of the darkness. Rob threw himself on to the floor. He rolled over. Then he saw a ghostly white face shining in the light.

Rob kicked out at it. He grabbed an empty box and threw it. His father groaned and got to his knees. Rob grabbed him by the shoulders and helped him to the hatch.

"Mum," he shouted, "help me get Dad down before it attacks again."

The beating noise came again from the blackness beyond the lamp. Rob ducked. He felt a rush of cold air.

"Quick. Help me get Dad down before it rips me to pieces," Rob screamed.

His mum grabbed his dad's feet. Together, they helped him down the steps.

"I'm going to call the police," his mother said. "They can sort out whoever it is."

"No," Rob told her. "There's no one in the loft."

"What do you mean, there's no one in the loft? Who hit your dad, then?" she asked.

"Not who. What. It was a bird. An owl," Rob explained.

"A what?"

"An owl. There's an owl in the loft."

She looked at him as if he was mad.

"Owl?"

"Honest. It attacked Dad, then it tried to get me. I saw it."

"That bang on the head has damaged your brain."

Rob's dad groaned and nodded his bleeding head. "Rob's right. There is a family of Barn Owls in the loft. I found them, then they attacked me."

With a look of horror on her face, Rob's mother shouted, "Get rid of them. I will not have them attacking everyone."

"You can't get rid of them!" Rob said.

"Just you watch me," she told him. "I'll do it myself."

"No," her husband told her. "It's not their fault. They have a nest up there with owlets in it. They only attacked to protect their young. If a giant walked into our house, we'd fight back."

"Speak for yourself, Dad. If a giant walked into our house I'd run a million miles," said Rob.

"But what about the noises Rob heard? The screams and the scraping at night?"

"I know why now," Rob said. "Barn Owls sleep during the day and hunt at night. They bring back live mice to feed their young. The screams I heard must have been the owlets playing with the mice before eating them."

"And how do you know that?" his mother asked.

Rob smiled. "We did all about it at school," he said.

"Then it's a pity you didn't think of that before you made up fancy tales about ghosts!" his mother told him.

Rob sneaked off to bed. He felt very foolish.